TURNING SKILLS, HOBBIES, AND YOUR PASSIONS INTO INCOME

THE ART OF PROFIT

CASH IN ON YOUR CRAFT

THE PROFITABLE PATH

DISCLAMER

This Ebook has been written to provide information about starting your own business using your skills, hobbies and whatever you have passion for. Every effort has been made to make this ebook as complete and accurate as possible. However, there may be mistakes in typography or content. Also, this e-book provides information only up to the publishing date. Therefore, this ebook should be used as a guide - not as the ultimate source.

The purpose of this ebook is to educate and does not warrant that the information contained in this Ebook is fully complete and shall not be responsible for any errors or omissions. The author and publisher shall have neither liability nor responsibility to any person or entity with respect to any loss or damage caused or alleged to be caused directly or indirectly by this e-book.

THE ART OF PROFIT
CASH IN ON YOUR CRAFT THE PROFITABLE PATH
TURNING SKILLS, HOBBIES & YOUR PASSION INTO INCOME

TABLE OF CONTENTS

SECTION 1: IDENTIFYING YOUR SKILLS, HOBBIES, AND YOUR PASSIONS
- Assessing your strengths: Recognizing what you're good at and what you enjoy doing.
- Exploring your hobbies: Delving into activities that bring you joy and fulfillment.
- Understanding your passions: Discovering the things that ignite your enthusiasm and drive.

SECTION 2: MONETIZING YOUR SKILLS
- Freelancing: Offering your skills on platforms like Upwork, Freelancer, or Fiverr.
- Consulting: Sharing your expertise with individuals or businesses in need of guidance.
- Teaching and tutoring: Providing lessons or workshops based on your skills.
- Creating digital products: Developing online courses, ebooks, or templates.

SECTION 3: TRANSFORMING PASSIONS INTO PROFITABLE VENTURES
- Writing: Publishing books, articles, or blogs on topics you're passionate about.
- Fitness and wellness: Becoming a personal trainer, yoga instructor, or wellness coach.
- Travel: Starting a travel blog, becoming a tour guide, or organizing travel experiences.
- Technology: Developing apps, creating software solutions, or offering tech consulting services.

THE ART OF PROFIT
CASH IN ON YOUR CRAFT THE PROFITABLE PATH
TURNING SKILLS, HOBBIES & YOUR PASSION INTO INCOME

TABLE OF CONTENTS

SECTION 4: MARKETING AND BRANDING YOURSELF
- Building a personal brand: Crafting a compelling narrative around your skills, hobbies, and passions.
- Creating a portfolio: Showcasing your work and achievements to attract clients or customers.
- Utilizing social media: Leveraging platforms like Instagram, LinkedIn, or TikTok to reach your target audience.
- Networking: Connecting with peers, mentors, and potential collaborators in your industry.

SECTION 5: OVERCOMING CHALLENGES & STAYING MOTIVATED
- Managing time effectively: Balancing your passion projects with other commitments.
- Dealing with rejection: Learning from setbacks and using them as opportunities for growth.
- Maintaining self-discipline: Developing routines and habits to stay focused and productive.
- Finding inspiration: Surrounding yourself with supportive communities and seeking inspiration from others' success stories.

SECTION 6: HOBBY TO HUSTLE MAKING MONEY DOING WHAT I LOVE
- Getting To Know Sam
- My Start & What I Have Acomplished
- What They Don't Tell You.. Don't Believe The Hype
- The Harsh Fact Of How It Really Is

INTRODUCTION

If you've been thinking about starting your own business or wanting to work from home and want to know how to really go about getting started without getting the runaround or scammed, I will share my story & what I learned and what I did to get started

You can start a business right now if you really want to there should be nothing stopping you from trying.

If you're like me, you know that hustling isn't just a word – it's a way of life.. As a Gen X woman from the vibrant streets of the Bronx, New York, I've been carving my own path as an entrepreneur since 2013, , navigating the ups and downs of being my own boss. And let me tell you, it's been one heck of a ride.

In our fast-paced world, the idea of turning your passion into profit isn't just a pipe dream anymore – it's a real possibility. That's why I'm excited to share this ebook with you. Whether you're a fellow hustler from the Bronx, a budding entrepreneur, or someone just looking to make a little extra cash, there's something in here for you.

Together, we'll explore how to take your skills, hobbies, and passions and turn them into income-generating opportunities. From freelancing to starting your own business, the possibilities are endless.

Now, what you're going to get in this E-book will be how to start a business yourself. The starter of how to get started along with helpful tools to start you in the proper direction.

So let's roll up our sleeves, tap into our creativity, and discover how to make our dreams a reality. Because in this world, there's no limit to what we can achieve when we hustle with heart. Let's dive in and make it happen.

SECTION 1

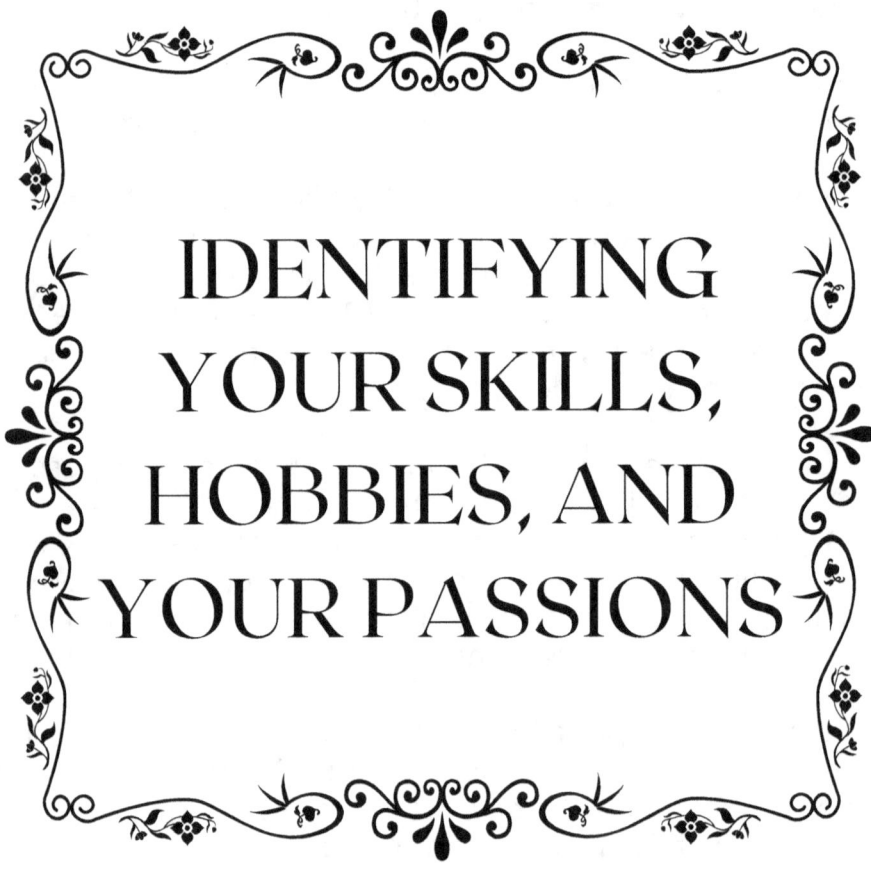

IDENTIFYING YOUR SKILLS, HOBBIES, AND YOUR PASSIONS

IDENTIFYING YOUR SKILLS, HOBBIES AND YOUR PASSIONS

Alright, let's get down to business and uncover what makes you tick – because trust me, there's gold in them thar hills! Identifying your skills, hobbies, and passions is the first step on the journey to turning your dreams into dollars. So grab a pen and paper (or your preferred note-taking device) and let's dive in.

Assessing Your Strengths: Recognizing What You're Good At and What You Enjoy Doing

First things first, let's take stock of your strengths. What are you naturally good at? Maybe you're a whiz with numbers, a wordsmith extraordinaire, or a master problem solver. Don't be shy – own your strengths! Reflect on past experiences, feedback from others, and moments where you've felt in your element.

For me, it was clear early on that I had a knack for connecting with people and a passion for storytelling. These strengths have served as the foundation for my entrepreneurial journey, shaping the way I approach business and interact with clients.

Now, think about what you enjoy doing. What tasks or activities light you up inside? It could be anything from organizing events to designing graphics to baking delicious treats. Remember, the key here is to focus on what brings you joy and fulfillment.

As a Bronx entrepreneur, I've discovered that combining my strengths with my passions has been a game-changer. By doing work that aligns with my natural talents and brings me happiness, I've been able to create a business that feels more like play than work.

Exploring Your Hobbies: Delving Into Activities That Bring You Joy and Fulfillment

Next up, let's talk hobbies. What do you do in your free time that makes you lose track of time? Whether it's painting, gardening, or playing an instrument, our hobbies often reveal hidden talents and interests that we may not have even realized we had.

For me, one of my favorite hobbies is cooking. There's something incredibly therapeutic about chopping vegetables and experimenting with flavors in the kitchen. my love for cooking has gives me the opportunity for me to cater events and host cooking workshops, If i choose to go down that path.

Another of my other favorite hobbies that im passionate about is digital art and creating images and quirky quotes. It's so satisfying to see my images and prints on different types of products and merch. And as it turns out, this love of creating digital art opened me up for unlimited opportunities in many different areas as a Freelance Graphic Designer.

So take some time to explore your hobbies. Try new things, get out of your comfort zone, and see what resonates with you. Who knows, you might discover a hidden talent or passion that could become the foundation of your next business venture.

Understanding Your Passions: Discovering the Things That Ignite Your Enthusiasm and Drive

Last but certainly not least, let's talk passions. What gets your heart racing and your pulse pounding? Your passions are the fuel that will drive you forward on your entrepreneurial journey, so it's crucial to identify what truly sets your soul on fire.

For me, one of my biggest passions is empowering others – particularly women of color – to pursue their dreams and reach their full potential. This passion is also another way I can profit, If I choose too!. It can open me up and led me to mentorship opportunities, speaking engagements, and collaborations with like-minded individuals who share my mission.

So think about what lights you up inside. Maybe it's advocating for social justice, creating art that sparks conversation, or building communities around shared interests. Whatever it is, don't be afraid to embrace it wholeheartedly.

Identifying your skills, hobbies, and passions is the first step towards building a business that not only pays the bills but also brings you joy and fulfillment. So take the time to assess your strengths, explore your hobbies, and understand your passions – because when you align your work with what you love, the possibilities are endless.

SECTION 2

MONETIZING YOUR SKILLS

MONETIZING YOUR SKILLS

Let's talk about the money moves – because let's face it, we all want to turn our skills into cold, hard cash. As a Gen X woman hustling in the Bronx, I've learned a thing or two about how to monetize my skills and expertise. So grab your hustle hat and let's dive into the world of making money doing what you love.

Freelancing: Offering Your Skills on Platforms like Upwork, Freelancer, or Fiverr

First up, freelancing. If you've got skills – whether it's writing, graphic design, coding, or anything in between – there's a demand for your services online. Platforms like Upwork, Freelancer, and Fiverr connect freelancers with clients from all over the world, making it easier than ever to find work and get paid for your expertise.

As a freelance writer, these platforms have been a game-changer for me. I've been able to land gigs writing articles, creating content for websites, and even ghostwriting books – all from the comfort of my own home. And the best part? I get to set my own rates and choose projects that align with my interests and expertise.

So if you've got a skill that people are willing to pay for, why not give freelancing a shot? It's a great way to dip your toes into entrepreneurship without taking on the full risk of starting your own business.

Consulting: Sharing Your Expertise with Individuals or Businesses in Need of Guidance

Next up, consulting. If you're a master in your field – whether it's marketing, finance, HR, or anything else – there are businesses out there who could benefit from your wisdom. Consulting allows you to share your expertise with others and help them solve problems, improve processes, and achieve their goals.

As a consultant, you have the flexibility to work with clients on a project-by-project basis or on a retainer arrangement. You can offer your services remotely or work with clients in person – whatever works best for you and your business.

Teaching and Tutoring: Providing Lessons or Workshops Based on Your Skills

If you've got a talent for teaching, why not monetize it? Whether you're a math whiz, a language guru, or a Photoshop pro, there are people out there who are eager to learn from you. Offering lessons or workshops based on your skills is a great way to share your knowledge with others and make some extra cash in the process.

You can offer one-on-one tutoring sessions, group workshops, or even online courses – the possibilities are endless. And thanks to platforms like Zoom and Google Meet, you can connect with students from all over the world without ever leaving your living room.

Creating Digital Products: Developing Online Courses, Ebooks, or Templates

Last but not least, let's talk about creating digital products. If you've got a wealth of knowledge and expertise to share, why not package it up into digital products that you can sell online? Whether it's an ebook, an online course, or a set of templates, digital products offer a passive income stream that can generate revenue while you sleep.

As someone who's dabbled in ebook writing, I can tell you firsthand that it's a great way to share your expertise with a wider audience and establish yourself as an authority in your field. Plus, once you've created and launched your digital product, you can continue to sell it indefinitely without any additional effort on your part.

Monetizing your skills is all about finding creative ways to leverage your expertise and make money doing what you love. Whether you choose to freelance, consult, teach, or create digital products, the key is to identify your strengths, find your niche, and hustle hard. So roll up your sleeves, put yourself out there, and watch the money roll in. You've got this!

SECTION 3

TURNING HOBBIES INTO INCOME STREAMS

TURNING HOBBIES INTO INCOME STREAMS

Whether you're a master baker, a green-thumbed gardener, or a crafting queen, there are plenty of ways to monetize your hobbies and turn your passion into profit. So grab your apron, dust off your camera, or pick up your paintbrush, and let's explore how you can make money doing what you love.

Arts and Crafts: Selling Handmade Goods on Platforms like Etsy or at Local Markets

If you've got a knack for crafting, why not turn your handmade creations into a profitable business? Whether you're into knitting, jewelry making, or woodworking, platforms like Etsy make it easy to sell your wares to a global audience. From unique jewelry to hand-painted ceramics to personalized gifts, the possibilities are endless.

As a fellow craft enthusiast, I've seen firsthand how lucrative selling handmade goods can be. I started out selling my crochet creations at local craft fairs and farmers markets, and before I knew it, I had a thriving online business with customers from all over the world. Plus, the satisfaction of seeing someone appreciate and cherish something you've made with your own two hands is priceless.

Photography: Licensing Your Photos to Stock Photography Websites or Offering Photography Services
If you've got an eye for capturing the perfect shot, why not turn your photography hobby into a money-making venture? Whether you specialize in portraits, landscapes, or food photography, there's a demand for high-quality images in today's digital world.

One option is to license your photos to stock photography websites like Shutterstock, Adobe Stock, or Getty Images. Every time someone purchases the rights to use one of your images, you'll earn a royalty fee – talk about passive income!

Alternatively, you could offer photography services for events like weddings, parties, or corporate gatherings. With the right equipment and skills, you can turn your passion for photography into a lucrative side hustle or even a full-time business.

Cooking and Baking: Starting a Catering Business, Selling Baked Goods, or Teaching Cooking Classes

If you're a whiz in the kitchen, there are countless opportunities to turn your culinary skills into cash. Whether you're a master chef or a home baker, there's a hungry market out there just waiting to sample your delicious creations.

One option is to start a catering business, providing delicious meals for events like weddings, parties, or corporate luncheons. With the right marketing and word-of-mouth referrals, you could soon find yourself booked solid with catering gigs.

Another option is to sell your baked goods at local farmers markets, food festivals, or online through platforms like Etsy or Instagram. From cookies to cupcakes to artisan bread, there's always a demand for homemade treats made with love.

And if you're passionate about sharing your cooking skills with others, why not teach cooking classes? Whether it's in-person workshops or online tutorials, teaching others how to whip up delicious meals is not only rewarding but also profitable.

Gardening: Selling Homegrown Produce or Offering Landscaping Services

If you've got a green thumb, there are plenty of ways to turn your love of gardening into a thriving business. Whether you're growing fruits and vegetables, cultivating beautiful flowers, or designing stunning landscapes, there's a demand for your expertise.

One option is to sell your homegrown produce at local farmers markets, community-supported agriculture (CSA) programs, or directly to restaurants and grocery stores. People are increasingly interested in buying locally sourced, organic produce, so there's a growing market for what you have to offer.

If you're more interested in the landscaping side of things, you could offer your services to homeowners or businesses looking to spruce up their outdoor spaces. From planting gardens to installing irrigation systems to designing outdoor living areas, there's no shortage of work for skilled landscapers.

Turning your hobbies into income streams is all about thinking outside the box and finding creative ways to monetize your passions. Whether you're into arts and crafts, photography, cooking and baking, or gardening, there's a world of opportunities waiting for you. So roll up your sleeves, get creative, and start turning your dreams into dollars.

SECTION 4

TRANSFORMING PASSIONS INTO PROFITABLE VENTURES

TRANSFORMING PASSIONS INTO PROFITABLE VENTURES

Alright, let's talk about turning those passions into profit – because trust me, there's nothing quite like making money doing what you love. Whether you're a wordsmith, a fitness fanatic, a wanderlust traveler, or a tech whiz, there are endless opportunities to turn your passions into profitable ventures. So let's dive in and explore how you can make your dreams a reality.

Writing: Publishing Books, Articles, or Blogs on Topics You're Passionate About

If you've got a way with words, why not share your thoughts, ideas, and stories with the world? Whether you're passionate about fiction, non-fiction, or poetry, there's a demand for compelling writing in today's digital age.

One option is to publish books on topics you're passionate about. Whether it's a novel, a memoir, or a self-help book, the publishing industry is always on the lookout for fresh voices and unique perspectives.

Another option is to write articles or blogs on topics that interest you. Whether it's travel, food, fashion, or personal development, there are countless websites and publications looking for talented writers to contribute content.

As someone who's been writing for as long as I can remember, I can tell you firsthand that there's nothing quite like seeing your words in print and knowing that you're making a difference in people's lives. So if you've got a story to tell or a message to share, don't be afraid to put pen to paper and start writing.

Fitness and Wellness: Becoming a Personal Trainer, Yoga Instructor, or Wellness Coach

If you're passionate about health and fitness, why not turn your passion into a profitable career? Whether you're into strength training, yoga, or holistic wellness, there's a growing demand for fitness and wellness professionals in today's health-conscious society.

One option is to become a personal trainer, helping clients achieve their fitness goals through personalized workout plans and coaching sessions. With the right certifications and experience, you can build a thriving business helping others get fit and healthy.

Another option is to become a yoga instructor, leading classes and workshops that promote physical, mental, and spiritual well-being. Whether you're teaching in a studio, at a gym, or online, there's a growing market for yoga and mindfulness practices.

And if you're passionate about holistic wellness, you could become a wellness coach, guiding clients on their journey to optimal health and well-being. From nutrition counseling to stress management techniques, there's no shortage of ways to help others live their best lives.

Travel: Starting a Travel Blog, Becoming a Tour Guide, or Organizing Travel Experiences

If you've got a case of wanderlust, why not turn your passion for travel into a profitable venture? Whether you're a seasoned globetrotter or a weekend explorer, there are countless ways to make money while seeing the world.

One option is to start a travel blog, sharing your adventures, tips, and insights with readers from around the globe. With the right niche and a unique voice, you can attract a loyal following and monetize your blog through sponsored content, affiliate marketing, and more.

And if you're passionate about creating memorable travel experiences, you could start your own travel company, organizing tours, retreats, and other immersive experiences for adventurous travelers. From culinary tours to wellness retreats to eco-friendly adventures, the possibilities are endless.

Technology: Developing Apps, Creating Software Solutions, or Offering Tech Consulting Services

If you're a tech-savvy entrepreneur, there's never been a better time to capitalize on the digital revolution. Whether you're a coding wizard, a UX/UI design guru, or a tech-savvy consultant, there are endless opportunities to turn your passion for technology into profitable ventures.

One option is to develop your own apps, creating solutions to solve problems and meet the needs of consumers in today's app-driven world. Whether it's a productivity tool, a gaming app, or a social networking platform, there's a demand for innovative and user-friendly apps in every niche.

Another option is to create software solutions for businesses, developing custom software applications, websites, or e-commerce platforms that help companies streamline their operations and achieve their goals. With the right skills and expertise, you can build a successful business providing tech solutions to clients in a wide range of industries.

And if you're passionate about helping others navigate the ever-changing world of technology, you could offer tech consulting services, advising individuals and businesses on everything from IT infrastructure to digital marketing strategies. With the right knowledge and experience, you can become a trusted advisor and help others harness the power of technology to achieve their goals.

Transforming your passions into profitable ventures is all about finding creative ways to monetize your interests and skills. Whether you're into writing, fitness and wellness, travel, or technology, there's a world of opportunities waiting for you. So don't be afraid to dream big, take risks, and pursue your passions with passion and determination. The sky's the limit, and the world is yours for the taking. Go out there and make it happen!

SECTION 5

MARKETING AND BRANDING YOURSELF

MARKETING AND BRANDING YOURSELF

Alright, let's talk about marketing and branding – because in today's digital world, how you present yourself to the world can make all the difference. Whether you're a seasoned entrepreneur or just starting out on your journey, building a strong personal brand is essential for attracting clients, customers, and opportunities. So let's dive in and explore how you can market yourself effectively and make a lasting impression.

Building a Personal Brand: Crafting a Compelling Narrative Around Your Skills, Hobbies, and Passions

First things first, let's talk about personal branding. Your personal brand is more than just a logo or a tagline – it's the essence of who you are and what you stand for. It's about telling your story in a way that resonates with your audience and sets you apart from the competition.

As a Gen X woman from the Bronx, your personal brand is uniquely yours. It's about showcasing your skills, hobbies, and passions in a way that reflects your personality and values. Whether you're a tech-savvy entrepreneur, a fitness enthusiast, or a travel junkie, your personal brand should convey what makes you special and why people should choose to work with you.

One way to build your personal brand is to craft a compelling narrative around your skills, hobbies, and passions. Share your journey, your experiences, and your expertise in a way that inspires and engages your audience. Whether it's through blog posts, social media updates, or video content, storytelling is a powerful tool for building connections and establishing credibility.

Creating a Portfolio: Showcasing Your Work and Achievements to Attract Clients or Customers

Next up, let's talk about creating a portfolio. Whether you're a writer, a designer, a photographer, or a consultant, having a portfolio of your work is essential for attracting clients and showcasing your skills.

Your portfolio should showcase your best work and highlight your achievements in a way that's easy to navigate and visually appealing. Whether it's a website, a PDF document, or a physical portfolio, make sure it's professional, well-organized, and reflective of your personal brand.

As someone who's been working for herself since 2013, I can tell you firsthand that having a strong portfolio has been instrumental in attracting clients and opportunities. Whether it's landing freelance gigs, securing speaking engagements, or getting featured in media outlets, my portfolio has been my secret weapon for standing out in a crowded marketplace.

Utilizing Social Media: Leveraging Platforms Like Instagram, LinkedIn, or TikTok to Reach Your Target Audience

In today's digital age, social media is a powerful tool for building your personal brand and connecting with your audience. Whether you're a social media maven or a complete newbie, leveraging platforms like Instagram, LinkedIn, or TikTok can help you reach your target audience and grow your online presence.

Choose the platforms that align with your personal brand and target audience, and focus on creating content that's engaging, informative, and authentic. Whether it's sharing behind-the-scenes glimpses of your work, providing valuable insights and tips, or showcasing your latest projects, social media is a great way to showcase your skills and connect with potential clients and customers.

As a Gen X woman from the Bronx, your unique perspective and experiences can help you stand out in a sea of sameness. Whether you're sharing your entrepreneurial journey, offering words of wisdom and encouragement, or shining a spotlight on fellow entrepreneurs and changemakers in your community, social media is a powerful tool for amplifying your voice and making a difference.

Networking: Connecting with Peers, Mentors, and Potential Collaborators in Your Industry

Last but certainly not least, let's talk about networking. As the saying goes, "it's not what you know, it's who you know." Building relationships with peers, mentors, and potential collaborators in your industry is essential for growing your business and advancing your career.

Attend networking events, join industry groups and associations, and connect with like-minded individuals online and offline. Whether it's grabbing coffee with a fellow entrepreneur, attending a workshop or conference, or joining a mastermind group, networking is a great way to expand your circle, learn from others, and uncover new opportunities.

As a Gen X woman from the Bronx, your unique perspective and experiences can make you a valuable asset to any network. Whether you're sharing your insights and expertise, offering support and encouragement, or collaborating on projects and initiatives, networking is a two-way street that can benefit both you and your peers.

Marketing and branding yourself is all about telling your story, showcasing your skills, and building relationships with your audience. Whether you're crafting a compelling personal brand, creating a portfolio of your work, leveraging social media to reach your audience, or networking with peers and mentors in your industry, the key is to be authentic, consistent, and intentional in everything you do. So roll up your sleeves, put yourself out there, and watch your personal brand soar to new heights. You've got this!

SECTION 6

OVERCOMING CHALLENGES AND STAYING MOTIVATED

OVERCOMING CHALLENGES AND STAYING MOTIVATED

Okay, let's talk about the real nitty-gritty – because being an entrepreneur isn't always sunshine and rainbows. From juggling multiple projects to facing rejection and everything in between, there are plenty of challenges that come with the territory. But fear not, fellow Bronx entrepreneur – with a little grit, determination, and a whole lot of hustle, you can overcome any obstacle and stay motivated on your journey to success.

Managing Time Effectively: Balancing Your Passion Projects with Other Commitments

One of the biggest challenges of being an entrepreneur is managing your time effectively. Between running your business, taking care of your family, and everything else life throws at you, it can feel like there just aren't enough hours in the day.

But fear not – with a little planning and organization, you can strike the perfect balance between your passion projects and other commitments. Start by creating a schedule that allocates time for work, family, self-care, and downtime. Prioritize your tasks based on their importance and urgency, and don't be afraid to delegate or outsource tasks when necessary.

As someone who's been working for herself since 2013, I can tell you firsthand that time management is key to staying sane and productive. Whether it's using a planner, setting reminders on your phone, or using time-blocking techniques, find a system that works for you and stick to it. With a little discipline and consistency, you can make the most of every minute and achieve your goals – one step at a time.

Dealing with Rejection: Learning from Setbacks and Using Them as Opportunities for Growth

Let's face it – rejection sucks. Whether it's losing out on a big client, getting turned down for a job, or facing criticism from peers, rejection can sting and shake your confidence. But here's the thing – rejection is not the end of the road, it's just a detour on the journey to success.

Instead of letting rejection knock you down, use it as an opportunity for growth and learning. Ask yourself what you can learn from the experience, how you can improve, and what you can do differently next time. Remember, every setback is a chance to become stronger, wiser, and more resilient.

As someone who's faced her fair share of rejection over the years, I can tell you firsthand that it's not always easy to bounce back. But by reframing rejection as a learning opportunity and focusing on the lessons learned rather than dwelling on the disappointment, you can turn setbacks into stepping stones toward success.

Maintaining Self-Discipline: Developing Routines and Habits to Stay Focused and Productive

As an entrepreneur, self-discipline is essential for staying focused and productive. Without the structure of a traditional 9-to-5 job, it's easy to get distracted and lose sight of your goals. But with the right routines and habits, you can keep yourself on track and make steady progress toward your dreams.

Start by establishing a daily routine that includes time for work, exercise, relaxation, and self-care. Set specific goals for what you want to accomplish each day, week, and month, and break them down into manageable tasks. Use tools like to-do lists, time-blocking techniques, and productivity apps to stay organized and focused.

As someone who's been working for herself since 2013, I've learned the importance of self-discipline the hard way. From resisting the temptation to procrastinate to staying motivated when the going gets tough, self-discipline is the secret sauce that separates successful entrepreneurs from the rest. So roll up your sleeves, set your sights on your goals, and stay disciplined – the rewards are well worth the effort.

Finding Inspiration: Surrounding Yourself with Supportive Communities and Seeking Inspiration from Others' Success Stories

Last but certainly not least, let's talk about finding inspiration. As an entrepreneur, it's easy to feel isolated and overwhelmed – but you don't have to go it alone. Surround yourself with supportive communities of fellow entrepreneurs, mentors, and like-minded individuals who can offer guidance, encouragement, and inspiration when you need it most.

Whether it's joining a mastermind group, attending networking events, or connecting with peers on social media, surrounding yourself with supportive communities can provide the motivation and accountability you need to keep going when the going gets tough. And don't be afraid to seek inspiration from others' success stories – whether it's reading books, listening to podcasts, or attending conferences, hearing about others' journeys can reignite your passion and remind you that anything is possible with hard work and determination.

In conclusion, overcoming challenges and staying motivated as an entrepreneur is all about resilience, resourcefulness, and a whole lot of hustle. Whether it's managing your time effectively, dealing with rejection, maintaining self-discipline, or finding inspiration, the key is to stay focused on your goals, stay true to yourself, and never give up on your dreams. So keep pushing forward, keep hustling, and remember – the best is yet to come. You've got this!

SECTION 7

HOBBY TO HUSTLE MAKING MONEY DOING WHAT I LOVE

A LITTLE ABOUT ME

Hello, to all my name is Samantha I hope all who are reading are doing well. I'm a Mom, a Friend and an Aspiring Entrepreneur a Spiritualist. I grew up in the hard streets of the Bronx, New York with a military mom and an older sister and life was not easy for me in any way shape or form. As I grew up and became a woman with a child of her own and a person who has gone through so many life struggles and still going through those life struggles.

My mind was set on trying to build a future for my son just like you and like many people, I started worrying about how I was going to put food on the table, pay rent and just to be able to live ect....
You know just the everyday life struggle we all go through while also dealing with the extra madness that life throws at us in the crazy unusual world we live in..

Life is surely a struggle and sometimes we don't know whether we are going left or right. Most of us think we got it all under control until one day something or someone proves us wrong.. Life sure threw all it had at me and sometimes I thought I wouldn't survive it. I lost so much and lost people I thought I wouldn't lose, especially myself. I watched the world go on without me and watch people change. around me and with me.

I just know I was at rock bottom. I allowed what life threw at me to knock me down. These knockdowns really were a struggle for me to get out of until I realized and not knowing I was suffering from Depression & Anxiety and was going through a Spiritual warfare I had no clue about. It made it 10x harder to pick myself up most of the time. My anxiety kept me homebound for almost 3 years and changed who I was completely.

Watching my loved ones work long hours and still not having enough money for what was needed, It really took a toll on all of us. Especially took a toll on me, I felt bad for not being able to help the way I wanted and the way they needed me, I started to feel like a burden.

It's that Moment when you really hit rock bottom, you end up slapping yourself in the face, self-reflecting, telling your own self to WAKE UP and do something about it because no one was going to do it for you. So, I decided to get up and to do something about it!

MY START

Back in the late spring early summer of 2013 I decided to hop online. I was dealing with a lot of family & relationship struggles and finding a job was like finding a needle in a haystack. I needed a distraction at the same time I needed to figure out a way to help out more. I started looking to find Legit opportunities I could try at a low cost. I was tired of living how I was and just watching the people I love live paycheck-to-paycheck and stressing about my situation or how something was going to get paid or how to keep a roof over my head or just money to have to buy and do stuff with my son.

I knew that there was something out there that would generate extra cash "than working long hours at a dead end Job. I knew with an online business I would be able to work anywhere and that all I needed was laptop/computer, Tablet or cell phone and a stable internet connection and would be able to spend more time with my son & imagined what it would be like waking up every morning, logging into my bank account and seeing money stack up because of all my hard work.

As I began my search I came across many opportunities, Most I tried and some I didn't bother with. Some opportunities worked and others didn't. I was new and didn't know what I was doing. I saw people making money from things that a child could probably do and I was struggling to make shit happen like most go through when we 1st start. So many people trying to make money online and so many people trying to get you to join them it was bananas.

There are millions of people trying to make money online but just don't know how to and lack the knowledge and training to get started. People investing their money into things that just make no sense and have nothing to offer or it being too complicated to understand or no one actually helping or not having money to get proper training.

This was my struggle.. I didn't get any real help nor was I mentored or guided. I had to learn gradually on my own without any knowledge or skills on how to go about it. So me not really knowing what to do & no one really wanted to help me, YouTube & Google became my best friends when those who promised to help didn't.

The Fear of being scammed or ripped off really made me & people hesitant to really try anything. Eventually I had to try and yes a few people scammed me but, it took me getting scammed for me to finally learn what opportunities were real and fake & what I really wanted to do.

In the process of me noticing that people failed to live up to their words and I saw many people like me struggling to find something that actually worked, I decided to take it upon myself and created a mission to help people look for affordable low-income opportunities even though I had no clue of what I was doing. People did come to me which made me know the time and effort I was putting was actually working for what I was doing at the time.

Everything is still a learning lesson & process and it will always be one, but, I'm glad I made that 1st step 10 years ago or I would not be here today writing about it.

My goal is to help as many people as possible because there are so many opportunities out there just waiting to be created. With the right mindset and motivation and effort anything can be achieved as long as you believe it can.

WHAT I HAVE ACCOMPLISHED

Now I'm not going not writing this book like I became a multi-millionaire and I got it all down packed, No I write this book in the realest way I can to show you that me being a female from the Bronx, New York who grew up in the South Bronx around drugs crime and violence among many other things that I have been through and dealt with so many obstacle in my life and still do that you can accomplish what you set your mind to.

In the past 10 yrs I have tried many opportunities I have tried many things like MLMs, Affiliate marketing, Membership websites-, Email marketing-, Direct Mail Marketing-, Video marketing,- Offering services,-Drop shipping- Direct sales- Apps Product Creations and from my own experiences it is very possible to make money from home. Now I could give you a list of names of all the opportunities I joined but we would be here forever.

One thing I used to do was revamp old opportunities. I used to create a better version of it, make them my own in some way and add more value than what was being offered from before. In doing that I realized that I wanted to build my own and be more creative and expressive. Many of those opportunities I tried did make me money, but not in the way I would have liked.

Since I didn't have the income coming in to really invest in myself to pay for tools or training or get the help Ii needed or got the bare minimum. I had to train and learn by myself.

I had to literally teach myself everything like how to market, how to build websites, create my own flyers etc And In doing so I picked up many different skills & talents along the way and learned that there were many ways to make money.

Now through my journey I have built many different avenues for me & In trying many things I found my passion. My passion was basically doing what I love to do and what mad eme happy. Now I have more than one business that I have been publicly putting out there, been making a name and branding myself for many of my skills, hobbies and passions.

Some of these skill, hobbies and passion are a homebased baker i love baking and cooking so decided to put myself out there when it came to my baking and cooking because your gir can cook her buttt off . I am also a handcrafter. I make homemade custom products jewerly, candles, oils, soaps and other goodies. I'm a Freelance Graphic Designer and I create designs, patterns, images & quotes for products & merch even created my own brand, more than one. & have created logos, flyers business card not only for myself but for other people as well.

Remember I'm just like you, with desires and passions, I'm not a guru or a multi millionaire, well not yet anyway. If I can create many avenues of income for myself with my skills, hobbies and passions, then why can't the next person. I told myself why wait till I make it to the top to share what I know when you can just join the journey if it leads you down that path to being your own boss and working to be financially free.

Starting my own Businesses and being my own boss was the best path for me because it allowed me to express myself in many ways and I found skills that I didn't know I posses and gained a liking to things I didn't think I would have liked or have an interest in.

I'm not here to try and convince you into anything. I'm here to provide you with a little knowledge & info and what you do with that Info is on you. My job is to pass it along and pay it forward and this is my way of doing that. By letting you know that is is possible to follow your passion and your dreams. It's upon you to take that step in the direction if you choose.

No one can direct or create your path only you can and with a lot of time and effort applied you can achieve anything in this world you put your mind too!

WHAT THEY DON'T TELL YOU
DON'T BELIEVE THE HYPE

Wouldn't you like to know when you join an opportunity that claims you can make this amount of money in this amount of time by doing this and that, But somehow seems to never work out how they say. You go and try one opportunity after another just to realize it's the SOSDDTS - Same Old Shit Different Toilet Smell that's what that abbreviates to.

Same BS info as the last. Showing you and telling you the same things no different from everything you have already seen, but leaving important and crucial details of how to actually achieve it. You've paid for multiple trainings saying the same thing but still not actually showing you the real deal, just only the BS that you can find for free on Youtube.

How many times have you purchased some kind of training or product and still have no idea how to actually go about making money with it. I know I have and still to this day there's few things I still don't understand and I won't sit here and write as if I mastered the way to success either that would be a lie. What most of these marketers are showing, the Big time and Small time marketers, are not Lies.

You can make money following what they do , but What they lack to do is to really lay down the nitty gritty of how they actually got there and basic explaining will not get us to where we want to be or where they have gotten to. Making us purchase training after training to still not fall into the same income bracket. Makes you mad, makes you discouraged and makes you just want to quit.. Why give us the BS just to put a dollar in their pocket. That's not how it should be.

They don't tell you that you need to have this & that in place. They don't tell you how hard it will be and most of the ones who claim to have made or make all this money definitely aren't really there to guide or mentor you properly. Most people take advantage of the fact that you're new to the online world trying to make some extra cash and will manipulate you to so many BS duplicated sites doing the same damn thing but make you believe they're different.

Such much fake crap goes on online and you really need to know when it's real and when you're being beat in the head with BS. This isn't everyone's cup of tea, coffee or cool aid and most won't drink not knowing the flavor 1st.
It's all about the Fear of Risk and taking that chance knowing failure can happen.

So Don't Fall for the Hype .. Some Hypes are true but most are Just Manipulations to get you to believe that's the income they're making and most are not making the amount of money they claim to be advertising about . Please don't be fooled with the BS but don't be hesitant either.

We will never know if something actually works until we actually try it. The issue is are you utilizing it the right way to get you to where you want? The majority of the time the answer is NO... That's because no one tells you the real deal. They just tell you the bare minimum.

We are adults and should be able to deal and make decisions. We have choices and it's up to us to decide what we will do about it no matter what the situation or circumstance are.

You want the truth well here it is .. Starting Your Own Anything Isn't Easy. It takes time, learning, persistence, effort, consistency, patience, & sometimes some investment. You may not need lots of cash but you will need some money to start off the correct way.

You need to actually put time into whatever it may be that you're trying to achieve. A computer, Laptop, Tablet or Phone and Internet connection isn't the only thing you will need to make money online.

If it was that simple we all would be making money now wouldn't we. Running a business no matter what field or niche it is in whether it's 1 or more, takes time, effort, patience and repetition. It really doesn't matter how many businesses or opportunities you try.

Nothing in life is easy & working from home is definitely not everyone's cup of tea, coffee or kool aid. Working from home takes courage and tough skin.

I say courage and tough skin because you can lose confidence and be discouraged at times when things are not working as planned when it comes to trying to work for yourself. You've got to really want this and want a better future for your family.

People are putting themselves out there and telling people who work a 9-5 that they can quit their jobs doing what they're doing, but yet they are still working a 9-5. How hypocritical is that? I would say very.

We need to stop the madness, stop the lies and the manipulations and start changing the way the games are played online and start showing a new way, Like the Truth. When you first start some people will luck out and have support & some will have less support then what you thought you had. You will actually see the true colors of people when you start working for yourself, when you're trying to make a difference for your family.

On this path to work for yourself to become your own boss, This journey will be hard to get yourself noticed, but it doesn't mean people don't see you. They do, they just don't know you to trust & what you're offering.

Very Hard Skepticism you will run into and in many ways, shapes and forms and that's what they don't tell you either. People online and offline can be rude and harsh critics & that's just the hard truth.!

If you don't have tough skin and a strong mind and will then just close the book now, But if you believe inside you know you got it in you then keep reading because as I share my experiences I also will be dropping some Tea on how you can start your own business and turn your skill, hobbies and passions into profit. The end game is worth it!

This book is not a guide on how to get rich fast there is no such thing unless you are doing something illegal. This is an I'm going to put effort into what I want and actually make it happen kind of like a guide book. Let me tell you this, You will lose friends, time & sleep to achieve this. If you really want to make something happen and work for yourself.

Those you lose in the process is because they're not meant to come on that journey with you. But as you lose you also gain & gain more than you lose.

Again its about letting of that Fear and taking the risk to go after your dreams your desires.
It's time to turn what you thought was nothing into something. Take the leap take the chance and believe in yourself that you can and it's possible.

THE HARSH FACT OF HOW IT REALLY IS

Is it possible to ditch your 9-5 to work from home? YES it is very possible , But this only happens once you have successfully established yourself as a known business or service or product, whatever you decided to go with that has been running for some time. Not for you to make a few dollars and think It's so simple as they make it seem. Creating a good business, service or product takes time & they're steps you must take to get there. You must know what you want to do before you even get started.

You're going to actually have to put in the work if you want to make something happen. You can do it if you put your mind into it, so you can start making the type of money that you desire. To have complete and total control over your life to do what you want, go where you want, when you want, with whoever you want without any limits.

This is all possible and here is the real harsh truth of what you need to do. Like I stated before, If you're looking for some "Get rich quick guide," or a way to take advantage of people and their money then please stop reading now. You will not get any of that here.

I created this to help empower people and lead people in the right direction that they are trying to get to. Now it is time to understand how this process of making money online works .

It took me over a few years to finally figure out how to actually achieve success online and make money for myself. A lot of sleepless nights, frustrations & struggles, blood sweat and tears is what it really takes to make it. You can't be a coward and give up when things get hard.

You will definitely have many discouraging days that make you just want to say Fuck it All, but you will also have a lot of good ones to that make you see and vision where you want to be and trying to get to. You will have many haters and people throwing negativity towards you, but if you let any of that get to you or turn you away then this Isn't The Cup Of Tea, Coffee or Kool Aid you want to be drinking.

CONCLUSION

As I reflect on my journey as an entrepreneur, I'm filled with a sense of pride and gratitude for how far I've come. Since 2013, I've been hustling, grinding, and paving my own path in the bustling streets of the Bronx, New York. And let me tell you, it hasn't always been easy – but it's been worth every ounce of effort.

Throughout the ups and downs, the victories and setbacks, one thing has remained constant – my unwavering determination to pursue my passions and turn my dreams into reality. From freelancing to starting my own business, from crafting a compelling personal brand to building a supportive network of fellow entrepreneurs, I've learned countless lessons along the way that have shaped me into the woman I am today.

As a Gen X Hispanic and Black woman, I've faced my fair share of challenges and obstacles on this journey. But with resilience, resourcefulness, and a whole lot of hustle, I've overcome them all and emerged stronger, wiser, and more determined than ever before. And while the road ahead may be long and winding, I know that as long as I stay true to myself, keep pushing forward, and never lose sight of my dreams, there's nothing I can't achieve.

So here's to the next chapter of my entrepreneurial journey – may it be filled with even more growth, success, and fulfillment than the last. And to all my fellow dreamers and doers out there, remember – the sky's the limit, and the world is yours for the taking. So keep hustling, keep dreaming, and never, ever give up. Because when you believe in yourself and your ability to make a difference, anything is possible.

Thank you for joining me on this journey. Here's to chasing dreams, breaking barriers, and making magic happen – one hustle at a time.

With gratitude and determination,
Samantha
https://linktr.ee/MzGo2Sa

www.ingramcontent.com/pod-product-compliance
Lightning Source LLC
Chambersburg PA
CBHW050028230526
45470CB00003B/1179